Let Go, Let God

By Jennifer M Maddy

Let Go, Let God

This book was first published in Great Britain in paperback during November 2022.

The moral right of Jennifer M Maddy is to be identified as the author of this work and has been asserted by her in accordance with the Copyright, Designs and Patents Act of 1988.

ISBN-13: 9798361278077

CONTENTS

Page

About the author

Jennifer M Maddy is a Qualified Reiki Grand Master Teacher and Practitioner.

IET (Integrated Energy Therapy) Master, Practitioner & Teacher.

Teacher of Rahanni Celestial Healing & other Healing Modalities.

Anchoring Spiritual knowledge & wisdom within every molecule of her being which enables her to reach higher dimensions of reality.

Special Needs Assistant (Inclusion Classroom Assistant) in St. Louis Secondary School, Dundalk for over 10 years.

This is Jennifer's 3rd book, her first 'Timeless love' and second 'We never say goodbye' have been well acclaimed, with numerous 5 star reviews on Amazon.

Regular workshops and healing sessions are held in Dundalk, Newry, Belfast, Dublin and surrounding areas. New Business called "INDEPENDENTLY TOGETHER" Holistic Practice Taking a holistic approach to a healthier, happier you!!

Holistic/Holism: The treating of the whole person including mental and social factors. A New way of thinking. We aim to educate children and adults on modern day holistic approaches to wellbeing.

Mindfulness Meditation, Sacred Sound Bath Healing, Reflexology, Talks, Goal Setting and Teaching the following different Holistic Modalities.

- **The Healing Angels of the Energy Field (Integrated Energy Therapy)** by Stevan J Thayer. Heart to heart healing. Learn how to establish an Angelic Heartlink to Ariel, Raphael, Gabriel, Celestina, Faith, Cassiel, Daniel, Sarah & Michael. One Day workshop with Sacred Sound by Brenda Coburn Murnaghan.

- **Basic Level of IET** (Integrated Energy Therapy) Opening the Channel of Compassion. The objective of IET is to provide a simple and gentle way to open the flow of Vital Life Force Energy within the human body and the human energy field by integrating suppressed feelings from the cellular memory and clearing associated energy blockages.

- **Intermediate Level of IET.** Learn how to clear emotional imprints from your Physical, Emotional, Mental and Spiritual Layers of your Human Energy Field.

- **Advanced Level of IET.** Bring your Soul's mission to life. Clear your resistance to Living your Soul's Mission. Align your Power and Build Spiritual Mastery.

- **Rahanni Celestial Healing.** From the Heavenly Dimensions of Reality. Healing for the heart from the heart. Rahanni Celestial Healing is something quite special and has been given to humanity as a Gift from

Source/God. Channelled by the 'higher-beings of love and light, to anchor an abundance of Light, Spiritual Knowledge and Wisdom into our aura to keep us as balanced as possible. Helps with ADHD and Ritalin. Great for children, bringing a better quality of life, helping to bring out and open them up to their natural essence of Truth, Love & Compassion. We are 'of one Heart' now and forever.

- **Dr Usui Grand Reiki Master Teacher.** Jennifer M Maddy & Brenda Coburn Murnaghan have completed Intensive Courses including practical theory & attunements in Dr. Usui Universal Healing Systems of Reiki Natural Healing to the 6th Degree, Grand Master Level guided & supported by Eileen McCourt, Reiki Grand Master teacher and practitioner.

- Reiki Seichem Master Teacher (Ann Watters)

- Reiki Master Teacher (Ann Watters)

- Fire Spirit Reiki Master Teacher

- Mary Magdalene Reiki Teacher

- Pyramid of Isis Reiki Teacher

- Seraphim Reiki Teacher

- Reiki Archangels Teacher

- Mother Mary Teacher

- Karuna - Prakriti Reiki Teacher

- Psychic Energy Surgery Healing Practitioner.

- Level 2 Diploma in Basic Reflexology Techniques, City & Guilds. Southern Regional College.

- Universal Reflexology.

- **Autism.** Introductory awareness of Autistic Spectrum Conditions. (Cache)

- **Sensory Processing** Disorder Course with Clare Educational Centre.

- Children's Workshops (Beams of Light) with Brenda Coburn Murnaghan.

Soul & Monad Mantra.
I am the Soul,
I am the Monad,
I am the Light Divine,
I am Love,
I am Will,
I am Perfect Design,
I am, I am, all that I am,
One with Universal Mind,
One with Source of all Life,
And they are one with me.
I am Love,
I am Light,
I am Peace,
I AM.

Acknowledgements

I wish to express my sincere and heartfelt gratitude to my wonderful family, friends, mentors and guides who encouraged and supported me on this path. Many roads have been travelled.

My Children, Adults now Leanne & Ben Sullivan. The Joy of My Life. Love you beyond words.

Don. Hale OBE and Dr Steve Green for their contributions.

David Connor, Brenda Coburn Murnaghan, Eileen McCourt, Declan Quigley, Kerry O'Hare and everyone who joined us during the year for all the lives we recorded for Facebook which ignited my Soul to write this beautiful book. We have had so many laughs along the way. It has been a great year of Soul Expansion. How blessed am I to collaborate with such highly evolved Souls. Together we are Stronger. Check out all of our Facebook pages. We hope that we are bringing some comfort and help to you during these times of change.

Thank you to all who attended our workshops, meditation circles, one to ones sharing your beautiful energies. We are all so blessed as our Soul Family grows. Thank you to everyone who contributed to this book. I am forever grateful.

Most of all, thank you Spirit, for all the messages and great blessings that are constantly being sent our way in this wonderful, loving, abundant universe.

Namaste!! And many Angel Blessings Always from our Hearts to Yours.

01112022 My late mum Teresa Maddy's 3rd Anniversary away from us, whom I again dedicated this book to. "Let Go, Let God". Thankyou, Thankyou, Thankyou. And so it is. Amen.

We Are One Breath, One Pulse, One Heartbeat beating together in Harmony.

Reviews

This is Jennifer's 3rd book, bearing further testimony to her own deeply-rooted and firm spirituality.

We are all One, - all the multitudinous and diverse dimensions that make up the entirety of Creation all inter-flowing, inter-mingling, inter-connecting and inter-dependent. We are all One in the One Great Universal Energy we call God. All the sky stuff, all the earth stuff, - all encompassing the same elements of Water, Air, Fire, Earth and Spirit. As the Metaphysical 16th century poet John Donne wrote: 'I am a little world made cunningly of elements and an angelic sprite.'

And this Great One Universal Energy, this One Great Universal Energy that flows thorough all things and in all things, - this is what we call God, the Great Universal Intelligence. And within this Great Intelligence, this One Great Universal Consciousness, even the humblest and tiniest creature has a contribution to make to the whole. It has life, it has a consciousness it has Spirit, - and Spirit is life, life is Spirit. We are all part of the great web of life, the great chain of being, all in the One Pulse, the One Heartbeat, the One Breath, - as Jennifer emphasises.

We all tend to go after our own outcome, and we pursue that relentlessly and ambitiously, ignoring the signs being constantly sent our way by this loving and providing Universe. But as this book emphasises, the Universe, - this Great Intelligence, - knows what is best for each and every one of us and what we need at any particular time that is for our Highest Good. So the message from this beautiful book is 'Let go and Let God'. Yes, by all means, send your request out there, but do not get attached to the outcome. Whatever you desire is already out there - let go and let the universe deliver! Go with the flow! Like the river, - the river does not try to knock down the tree in its path, it just flows around it.

This book is not just a one-read, but a handbook that you will keep beside you and return to through your daily life. It explains that the most important relationship you will ever have in your life is your relationship with yourself. We are all here on a Soul Mission, we all have a great contribution to make, and we all have a bright light to shine. Everything we do, everything we say, - all creates a ripple that goes out beyond us to all of Creation. And even though we are all One, there is uniqueness in diversity, - as Jenny explains, we are 'independently together'.

This book is for everyone, - everyone that is who is intent on advancing on their spiritual path. There is no such thing as chance or coincidence - there is only synchronicity, - synchronicity being when all the necessary elements come together in the universe in order to produce a certain outcome, - and everything happens in divine timing and not in our timing. And there is a time for everything. In particular a time to let go! A time to let go of all that no longer serves you on your spiritual path.

Let this beautiful book guide you through your daily life. It is full of positive affirmations, meditations, and words of guidance from Archangels, many Higher Beings of Light and from Mother Earth. It teaches that to thrive and not just survive in this troubled world, you need to set your soul free, - and you set your soul free by surrendering the need for control - 'Let go and let God'. Come out of your head, which is so much controlled and manipulated, and reconnect with your own heart and your own Higher Self, which is you in your pure, undiluted God Essence. That is who you really are!

A beautiful, inspiring book. Congratulations, Jennifer!

Eileen McCourt,

Spiritual author and teacher. www.celestialhealing8.co.uk

'Let Go, Let God, is a beautiful snapshot into an ordinary life, not without its struggles, pain, hurt and disconnection, but despite the difficulties, we see a person choosing to rise, to heal and step into their power. In many ways, this is a routemap for hope, for meaning and for a deep spiritual understanding. Following on from Jennifer's previous book, 'Timeless Love ', we see a deepening and widening of her spiritual path, continuing to discover the true nature and wonder of this life... and God, freed from the choking stranglehold of organised religion. Rather than be content to dwell in spiritual mundanity, Jennifer is moving forward, discovering new pathways to God, new energies, new healing. 'Let Go, Let God' is a timely reminder of the necessity to fully inhabit our own lives, give thanks and move forward. Jennifer is someone taking responsibility for her life, her spirituality and her role in the Universe, finding and redefining her Soul purpose. A lesson to us all. Quite simply, this book is full of hope, full of meaning, full of the joy of spiritual discovery. A book that brings light to these very dark times.

Declan Quigley

Shamanic Practitioner and Teacher, Anam Nasca Shamanism

Lots of inspirational gems of insight from the beautiful and authentic Jennifer Maddy. Jennifer embodies all that she has written in this book, as it comes from her life experiences. She uses stories from her personal life to serve as inspiration and shows strength in her openness and vulnerability.

The book is also peppered with relevant quotes from other healers, Angels and Jennifer's own spirit guides to add variety and a broader perspective. It is humility to acknowledge and honour the gifts of others that makes Jennifer a beacon of love and respect in her community and beyond.

For those starting out on their spiritual awakening, it would serve you well to learn from those who have paved the way for you. Jennifer is one of those leaders and her words of wisdom serve as a blueprint for spiritual guidance.

Much love and blessings Jennifer,

Shane Donohoe – 'Celtic Shaman'

Introduction

"Angels with me Every day, listen closely While I Pray"

This is my Bible. My God Box. My Beliefs. I trust the messages I receive from God and his messengers. I sincerely hope my words resonate with some of you.!!!! God in essence is Good energy. I myself am lucky to hear messages from my Spirit Team (my higher self) and I trust the words and messages that are given to me. My mum always said, you don't need to go to mass or church to talk to God, have direct communication and enjoy your own relationship with him/her. She had great faith and said the rosary everyday when she was out

1

walking. She believed in the power of prayer, especially the rosary, and handed this teaching down. She never pushed her views on us and we now are able to make up our own minds and form our own beliefs.

We all have a gift and the ability to tap into a higher consciousness. Over the past years, I have studied a lot of courses on Holistic practices, reflexology, ki energy massage, Indian Head massage, different healing modalities especially IET (Integrated energy therapy, Reiki, Rahanni Celestial Healing. I gathered information on different world religions and understandings and integrated their energy into my being. Allowing diversity and listening to different peoples points of views I believe I Am All-Inclusive in my faith and beliefs.

And most importantly noticing the signs that the Universe puts in front of me, which are put on my path alone. Everyone walks their own path. We are all unique and individual. Personally, I love learning and every day is a school day here on Earth. Every experience is a lesson, good and bad. It's all part of the great web of life. Every person we encounter is part of our awakening. Every moment is precious. "If we don't climb the mountain, we won't see the View. "Climb to new heights and accomplish new dreams and goals.

We just need to become conscious and wake up. Live in the present moment. And the Golden Rule, I believe is Love (treating others as one wants to be treated).

All these experiences have helped me to believe and trust in myself. I have confidence now to share some of my messages and stories.

God is seen as being Trinity in Unity. We are not separate from one another, We are One.

As I sit here in God's waiting room metaphorically (my life) knowing life was never supposed to be a waiting room, writing and reflecting for my Third Book, I realise that the most important relationship in your life is your relationship with SELF. Everything else on the outside is a reflection of your inner world.

Sometimes in life we feel a little bit broken, as if our wings are damaged. A little bit lonely and sad, wondering Why Me?

And my Answer is Communication.

Communication has broken down, yet again in my life. I have pulled away and retreated into my own shell. Just like a hedgehog in hiding. Feeling safe in my own darkness, in my own cocoon, as I retreat.

It's ok to retreat, to hide away, to go within. To drop into the cave of your own existence and rest for as long as it takes. No rush, no pressure, no expectations, no limits on Time, When or How.

Feeling into your own Emotions and understanding your pain, your feelings, your thoughts, your words and actions.

For me, Journaling, writing and expressing from the depths of my Being.

Being Present to my own Presence and giving myself time to surrender and acknowledge, Who I am, As I let Go, Let God. There is no right or wrong, there is no blame or doubt. Communication is communion with yourself, Higher Self, your Guardian Angel, Angels, Archangels, Spirit Guides, Lineage of Ancestors who have walked before you, your family and friends who have passed to Spirit, leading Lighting the Way home and of course earth angels who cross our paths.

Take time to connect to your past, your life, your experiences, good, bad and ugly and fully integrate all aspects of yourself for growth, soul expansion. Know that you are truly loved and surrounded by a warm cocoon of Unconditional Love. Sometimes, I am afraid to verbally speak my feelings to another person. I find if I write a letter to them from my heart to theirs, it releases the stagnant energy that holds me back. I don't have to give the person the letter. My Intention is enough. They receive the message telepathically in divine timing. And I have released the worry from my consciousness. Have you ever just thought about someone, and the phone rings and it's them on the phone.

I also write love letters to Spirit. People who have passed on, family members and other spirits that come into my awareness. I tell them how much I love and miss them and if I have never met the spirit before (passed loved one who wishes to connect), it begins our relationship. Opening the channel of communication. I also write letters to new people I have yet to meet in the future. This attracts their energy to you. This is fun and brings into your awareness new people, places, settings and situations before it manifests itself. Message in a bottle.

1. Unconditional Love

Unconditional Love. Love without Conditions.

When you are fully accepted for Who you Are. Not judged. Fully understood and accepted. Fully free of responsibility and not dependent on pleasing or giving to others. Respected and valued by others for your soul qualities of your spirit and not your downfalls or what you own, material belongings. We come into this world with nothing and we leave the world with nothing. It's the impact of love we leave behind along the way that is important.

Taking back your Power and committing to Love, Honor and Respect yourself. Honouring your Body, your Mind and your Soul. Entering into Godhood/Goddesshood. And pray tell, how do we do that? You align and balance your chakras (the energy centres in your body falling into your soul consciousness. Communicate with the cells in your body and uncover the blueprint of your DNA.

Asking yourself, How may I serve Humanity? How can I express myself, live my life fully in service to God and to Man, Woman, Child, Plant, Animal, Mother Earth. Every living being. opening up to beingness.

Be a Conduit for the Divine manifestation into form. Knowing everything is perfect, just as it is. Everything is blessed and sacred and happens in Divine Order, Divine Plan, Divine Timing. DIVINE INTEGRATION for your

Crystal Clear Pure Reflection of yourself. Trusting the process. Awaken to the Truth, Love and Compassion that you are here to express.

Opening up your 6th Sense. See, hear, taste, smell, feel, sense, touch, breathe. One Breath, One Touch, One Heartbeat.

ONENESS

All Dimensions.

Opening the Veil to your Higher Self.

2. Energy

A little bit about my previous books and how I integrated their Energy into my Work from my True-Life Experience. Everyone has a Story. I Choose to let go of beliefs that need to be healed and forgiven. We get to choose if we are a victim or survivor and transmit a frequency, a vibration (An Energy Field of Colour in our Aura)

What is your Story?

Now my story is, I have two grown up children, adults now, whom I adore and I am so proud of and their partners. I am in long loving relationships. A loving family circle and friends. Trustworthy relationships that I value. I still have to do work everyday to make these relationships work.

I have 4 dogs and my son's dog Ozzy comes to visit which makes 5. The best companions of all. I think I am known now as the mad dog woman. I feel like my home is a dog hotel as everyone leaves her dogs here. God in reverse is Dog. My daughter has 2 rabbits, 3 hens, 2 cats and her best friend, her horse Ted ((Teddy bear) and a new addition to our family Polly a Falabella pony. And I look forward to my grandchildren in the future.

I AM now a Master Teacher in IET (integrated energy therapy) and a Grandmaster Teacher in Reiki and work with Universal Reflexology, Unicorn Reiki Practitioner,

Pegasus Reiki Master Practitioner and other healing modalities. I Teach these beautiful healing modalities around Ireland, worldwide and online. I absolutely love my work and I have pride and passion in helping other people evolve. This is part of my Souls Mission. Every time I received an initiation/ attunement during a course, its energy reflected back in my life.

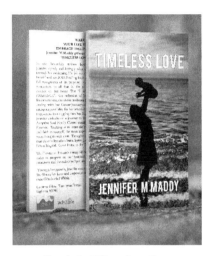

Book 1. "Timeless Love

This is my life story. How I became an Energy Healer and uncovered my roots to build solid foundations. On reflection, in my opinion, this book reminds me of the Basic Level of IET (integrated energy therapy) and the first degree in Reiki. A lot of healing took place in this book through my own spiritual journey and rebirth. I am grateful for all the lessons learned and the people who graced my path. Family and friends. Thankyou from the bottom of my heart.

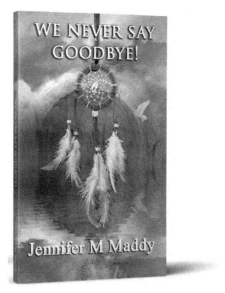

Book 2. "We Never Say Goodbye"

When writing this book, I asked the 9 Healing Angels of IET to bring together true-life stories from genuine people expressing how they awakened to their Souls Calling, through writing about their true experiences that helped transform them. These people are my family, friends, mentors, guides and life long relationships. We will always be connected.

It reminds me of the Intermediate Level of IET (Integrated energy therapy), 2nd degree in Reiki & learning Universal Reflexology. The chakras in our feet correspond to every organ in our body. Every chakra has a colour. Red, Orange, Yellow, Green, Blue, Indigo and Violet. The Colours of the Rainbow. Sole to Soul Healing. Every chakra holds an energy and emotion, and by energising, triggering and releasing negative emotions that are held in the body, we integrate new positive energy.

We are the Change. So grateful and thankful to everyone who took the time to contribute to this book. Together we are strong.

I also write about the Angelic number 222 energy which prompted my writing of this book. Message from my late mammy Teresa Maddy as she gently took her last breath and transcended to the Spiritual Realm.

Trust that everything is working out exactly as it's supposed to be, with Divine Blessings for everyone involved. Release and let go of anything that does not serve you anymore, for your highest good and highest healing. Transmute energy with the Angels of the Violet Flame. Let Go Let God.

222. Find peace, even in times of struggle. Good things are on their way if you trust and believe. Predestined Life. Pure Destiny.

Letting Go.

No relationship is all sunshine and rainbows but people can share one umbrella to survive the storms together. Together we are stronger.

Poem about the Feet. (Soul to Sole Reflexology)
Given as a gift from Paula O'Hare, Warrenpoint.

Give me your feet and they will reveal.
The pains and traumas that you feel.
Let me massage and gently press
And try to release your inner stress

Give me your feet and we will commune
Together we will hear the body's tune.
If there's a note that is off key.
We'll tune it in and set it free.

Give me your feet - I'll set the pace.
While you relax in your own secret place.
We'll access energy and block 's release.
And reinstate your inner peace.

Thank your feet for supporting you well.
And listen to the tales they tell.
In a subtle way your feet can talk.
And help us enjoy the path we walk.

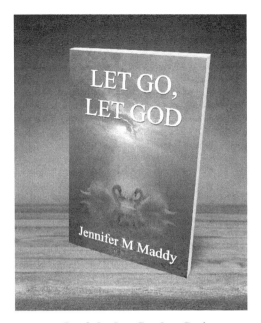

Book 3., Let Go, Let God

This book reminds me of the 3rd degree in Reiki and the Advanced Level of IET (Integrated energy therapy) and Rahanni Celestial Healing. Angels of the Violet Flame. Healing modalities that I teach. I love working with the 9 Healing Angels of IET. Each angel works on the 7 main energy chakras in the body. During the Advanced level we teach how to reach the Energetic potential of your Souls Mission.

Embrace your Souls Mission.

Envisioning

Enact your Souls Mission.

We in essence, must ground our Divine Spark into the Earth in order to manifest our vision and bring our Souls mission to Life. Remember everyone is unique and we all connect by a chain of life. We are all individuals, and no one is more important than the other. We all have a Basic human right for survival, dignity and moral responsibility.

We are One Breathe,

We are One Pulse,

We are One Heartbeat.

"We don't have to know where you are going, as long as you know you are on your Way" Stephen J Thayer.

Mantra "I respectfully demand that I communicate my feelings, my thoughts, my words to release and let go of stagnant energy and emotions that no longer serve me NOW"

DIVINE INTEGRATION

This is a Beautiful CD composed by myself and Brenda Coburn Murnaghan, my business partner who is also a Grand Reiki Master like me. We work in harmony together and combine our skills to enhance our work. It's fantastic to have help and we encourage and push each other to reach our full potential. We hold mediation evenings in our local area which are a huge success. We also teach healing modalities together as we are both passionate about our work and its power to change people's lives. We have gained great strength and wisdom over many years of working together to share. (Share our Love)

Disk 1: Guided Meditation

This divine light meditation raises your vibration and brings you into full alignment. Connect to your Higher self and Source Light Energy. Illuminate your Souls Destiny. Stop doing, relax and just BE and bathe in Spiritual Alchemy.

Disk 2. Sacred Sound Bath

Immerse yourself in the sounds of Tibetan Bowls, Gongs, Shamanic Drums, Shanti Bells and Chimes. Allow the tones and vibrations of these wonderful sounds to bring you on a deep journey of relaxation and meditation. Sound Healing has been known to aid in stress relief, anxiety attacks, depression and other mental and physical issues, whilst promoting a much improved sleep pattern. Relax and allow the sound to immerse your whole being.

3. The Choice

"Even in hell, hope can flower" Edith Eger.

Believe in Life, not Loss, Believe in Life means it's ok to Let Go, Let God.

We can trust where we have been, where we are going and know we are right where we need to be right Now.

Glow your True Colours.

SAY: Lord help me do your Will.

DO: Make a donation, or give time to a charity that works to promote Justice, Peace, Integration. Love.

PRAY: Communion Together.

Energy Follows Intention. When we pray together and pray for each other we unite together as one. Talk to God, your angels and Ask for help and advice. Give out to God. Shout out loud when you are angry or frustrated. Scream. Be honest. Feel your emotions.

MEDITATE: An Inward Prayer. Uncover the Truth of your Soul. Listen to your own INTUITION. Unlock the key and knowledge that is held deep in your heart and Soul, buried over many lifetimes.

LEARN: Be a prophet. Speak for God.

"If we don't listen to that voice of God, telling us to "GO" we will risk a life lived in second gear." President Obama

When we feel stuck in life as if we have hit a brick wall, trapped by circumstances, anxious, depressed, bored, uneasy, not excited by everyday chores and interactions, it could be a signal that it's time to change something. Change can often feel as though you are out of control, falling out of your comfort zone and scared. It's ok to feel this way sometimes, we all do. Let the negative aspects of yourself release and in doing so you will eventually feel your tower of strength reappear. Don't wait to get sick before you decide to change. Read ("Timeless Love"), my first book reflecting on my Cancer Experience) Change NOW Try to get out into nature, clear your head, eat healthy, drink plenty of water, exercise and change the vibrations that are being held in your mind and body. Begin a new chapter in your life. Close the current chapter and begin again. Everyday, we are given a blank canvas and a clean slate to start again. One step at a time. Meditate and listen to that voice of God within, telling you to move. Make a choice, take a chance to make a change, or change will never happen." Speculate to accumulate. "Become a VIP in your life. (very important person) You are responsible for your own life. No one else's. Be so busy living that you do not have time to worry about anyone else 's business.

Listen to your heart, connect your mind and live from your Soul and follow your Soul's calling. Build solid foundations. Sometimes the paths we walk can become rocky and unbalanced. We forget Who We Are and Why We Are Here. Uncovering your roots, your family tree and discovering where your Ancestors came from is sometimes necessary to paint a full picture in your mind and helps you to understand more fully your inherited traits. Every family has history, either good or bad. It's learning to accept all of ourselves, our shadows as well as our light, and choosing to love each person for the bright spark of divinity that dwells inside them.

Recently I got a nudge and travelled to England to reconnect with my birth family again. I met up with my Birth Dad, Anthony Power, his wife Mary and daughter Katrina. Katrina is confined to a bed. She lost oxygen at birth and had a seizure at a young age. She is now 33 years old. Because of this, her life changed from being a healthy child to an adult experiencing physical problems. She couldn't talk and kept smiling at me. This melted my heart. I know telepathically, she knew who I was, her sister. I held her close and kissed her hands. I promised to visit her in my dreams so we could go dancing together. It's amazing how we can experience these outer body experiences, once we put our mind to them. We will have our own relationship through telepathically connecting. So grateful and humbled to have been in her company. Life changing.

My advice to everyone is please don't wait until it's too late to tell someone that you love them. Tell them today. Show kindness, and leave sparkles of love wherever you go. And if you physically can't meet up, Shout your Love out to the Universe. The Universe will respond to your call. Heart to heart connection. A great movie I watched years ago was the Celestine Prophecy. It's truly amazing what we can do with the power of our minds and energy.

The next day I met up with my sister Kerry on my birth mum's side of the family. We had such fun and chatted about our families and childhood memories. Kerry gave me a gift of a picture with my Birth mum Kitty in it. She looked so beautiful with the light clearly around her. Kerry also gave me a little necklace with the tree of life. Such beautiful treasures to take home. It's the little things in life that matter the most. Priceless.

Unfortunately, I did not get to meet up with everyone in my family on this trip and hopefully I will return again soon and keep all of these relationships alive. We have to make a conscious effort to work on relationships.

Cricklewood Church (Photo by David Connor)

We visited the local church in Cricklewood as it was my birth mum's anniversary on the 15th August. 2022.

I had written a letter to my Birth mum years before which I found in an old diary which I wrote in 2010.

Dear Kitty O'Sullivan.

My beautiful birth mum in heaven without whom I would not be here.

When I was a baby in your womb, I could feel, hear, touch and smell you. I was connected to you by our Souls. You give me the gift of life and I am forever grateful. I forgive you for letting me go as you had no other choice and today I reach out to thank you. I am who I am today through God's Power, he has opened my eyes to see, opened my ears to hear. Opened my heart to heal. Opened my hands to touch and share my love. I am the perfection of Life. Your life lives on through me.

Thankyou from the bottom of my heart.

Your daughter,

Jennifer

I know my birth mum had to give my brother Matt up for adoption as well. This must have been horrendous for her. Very hard times back in the 1970;s. We have reconnected again on a recent visit to Murcia and Alicante in Spain. I was overwhelmed with so much love on this trip from everyone. Thank you. xxx

Matt and I were walking down a little street and a woman was walking in front of us wearing a dress with the message written on the back. Disconnect to Reconnect. What a message our mum gave us. Taking time out from our everyday lives to spend family time together with loved ones we cherish.

I will share another letter that I wrote back in 2015 which I found in another diary.

Dear Future Husband.

Here are a few things I'd like to say. Please treat me like a lady....

Please love and respect me for who I am and please don't try to change me. I may not be perfect, but parts of me are pretty spectacular.!!!! I look forward to meeting you and building our relationship together.

Thankyou with love in my heart to your heart.

Jennifer.

A beautiful song my late darling mammy Teresa Maddy sang to me as a child growing up was

"Nobody's Child" by Daniel O'Donnell. I could have been that child as I was adopted and left in a basket waiting to be chosen by my Soul Family. From my First Book "Timeless Love" I explain more about my journey and uncovering my Roots. This journey has mapped me into the Beautiful Woman I AM today and I am tremendously grateful and forever humble.

The Late Denis and Teresa Maddy. My mammy and daddy. My rocks in life and in Heaven. Always with me, cheering me on from the sidelines.

4. Open your Cosmic HEART

Open your cosmic heart. Let Go, Let God and radiate light.

Allow Energy to flow into every organ, every cell and every fibre of your being.

Breath into this awareness. Energise and revitalise.

Divineness/Humanness/Wholeness.

Appreciate YOU. Unconditional Love, no Conditions.

Invest in yourself through learning healing modalities that help you grow and heal before choosing to attract relationships that honour your Soul, especially if you have been hurt before in previous relationships that honour your Soul, especially if you have been hurt before in previous relationships. Either platonic or sexual. You may find it hard to trust and move forward again. Attract relationships that feel natural. Where you have empathy for each other. You respect each other and share similar life goals. Attract relationships that challenge you in order for your soul to grow and expand. Relationships that motivate you, where you feel inspired. Learn how to compromise and talk about your issues from a place of truth and honesty. Be willing to take steps to improve your relationships and choose to become a better person. Relationships that are passionate and exciting. Be each other's fans. Their wins are your wins. Their losses are your losses. Feel each other's pain. Love everything about each other without Condition.

My own personal relationships are not perfect by any means, believe me. They are a work in progress. I don't have a good track record. I think that's why I can relate to this topic! When I sat down to write this book, I questioned myself, How can I write a book about relationships?" Why not, spirit said!!!!

Relationships are aligned to your Soul. Within your heart you hold a Compass, your Souls GPS. Trust the vibes you get when you meet someone. You will feel their energy first and determine whether this vibration is your soul reflection. Be Crystal Clear from the start and cut out the bullshit. You will save yourself time and energy. Feel and respect each other's presence. Heart to heart. Soul to soul. "Oh Sacred Heart of Jesus, I place all my trust in you.". Trust is the key in relationships. Speaking your truths from a place of vulnerability and not being afraid of being authentic. Admit when you are wrong and move on. Forgive yourself for your mistakes. We are human and not perfect. We are perfect in our imperfections. Compromise in relationships and be gentle with each other. If we didn't make mistakes we would never learn. Listen to your own heart and intuition first. Don't keep asking other people for advice as no one knows what your soul agreement and plan is. Sometimes you stay in relationships longer than necessary until you learn the lesson that you are here to learn and trust your own inner guidance.

Learn what is sacred, Yes and No where you listen to your soul nudge. A feeling you get in your gut and body. It honestly takes time to trust your soul whispering and understand how to interpret and understand it. It's like exercising your muscles in the gym to get stronger and fitter. It does not happen immediately. It takes patience, time, energy and commitment. Every day, make a conscious effort to understand yourself and your soul's calling.

In our modern world, life has gotten so fast, so materialistic. We need to strip back the layers and come back to basics. Simplicity. Appreciate all you have. A grateful Heart is the most abundant. We need to live under one umbrella supporting each other.

5. Do you LOVE Yourself?

Anything that irritates you is teaching Patience.

Anyone who abandons you is teaching you Independence.

Anyone that angers you is teaching you compassion.

Anyone that has power over you, is teaching you to be Sovereign.

Anything you hate is teaching you Unconditional Love (Love without Conditions) Anyone who makes you feel fearful is teaching you Courage.

Anything you can't manage is teaching you to Surrender (Let Go, Let God).

Love Letters.

See the Universe as a personal love letter written by the Divine to you. Please review from your throne that if God is love and you are God essence, he is sharing his love with you right NOW, so he shares his ultimate power with you. Feel love spreading through your whole universe from his heart to yours.

"Dear God, Where are you? A bewildered Soul talks with God", by Eileen McCourt.

What is LOVE????

Love is a vibration, an essence. It transcends all time and space. When we fall out of love with someone, it means we are no longer vibrating at the same frequency. Our Soul's lesson has been completed and it's time to move on to new soulmates/friends. This chapter of our life has been written in our Soul's contract before we were born. So we accept what is, let go of what was, and move forward. This movement allows our Soul to expand and grow. There is no fault or blame, it's time to allow new energy in. Sometimes we are hard on ourselves and hold unforgiveness in our hearts towards the other person. This energy does not serve us. Let go, Let God of stagnant emotions. Let go of guilt and pain. Live from your own truth and integrity and trust your ability to know what is true for yourself. Embrace change and forgive yourself first, the most important person in your life and then the other person. Set your Soul free.

Only Love is Real. (A Course in Miracles). Everything else is an illusion. Share your Love.

Be Love. Know you have no needs. Everything is supplied. Love transforms all negativity. Learn that you don't have to do anything or go anywhere to have amazing experiences, connect to your Higher Self. Focus on the experience of watching the higher power or God.

Trust.

"I Love YOU" means "I don't want to change or control you. I love you for your differences and diversities. I do not judge you. I see the light within you. You can be vulnerable and show me your true essence.

We are all One.

Unified in diversity, oneness and uniqueness. Allow your divine light to shine bright. Tune into your breath. Listen to your heart, Beating in unison to the sound of time. The time is NOW. It's an experience that transcends the mind. Feel one with everything and everyone. We are all Connected.

REFLECTION: Love, Loyalty & Friendship.

Sovereignty, Integrity, Truth & Compassion. Embody these qualities within to attract them.

You can spend your whole lifetime looking for love. Love will find you when you least expect it. Long term relationships need healthy "Immune Systems" that cope with inevitable stresses that arise between individuals for longevity. Healthy in body, mind, soul and spirit. All in balance. A juggling act that takes effort for all parties concerned. Plenty of patience & understanding, which are probably the hardest emotions to master, in my own opinion. Lol.

Mandra. I place my heart in the hands of God, and I trust God to place my heart and hands into the relationships that honour my Soul.

First, Self Loving Self.

Love yourself for what you know and don't know.

Love yourself for who you think you are and who you think you are not.

Love yourself to the moon, the stars in the sky and all the way beyond and back.

Love yourself for the light that you are, bigger and brighter than you know.

Love yourself through thick and thin and everything else in between.

Love yourself, just where you are and embrace the certainty of who you are BECOMING.

Love yourself and your uniqueness, there is no one quite like you.

Love yourself for the treasure that you are, the priceless unpolished Diamond Heart that is you.

Love yourself back to aliveness and embrace the timely awakening of you. Love yourself back to LIFE.

6. Soul Plan

The creativity of the Universe flows through me as I focus my thoughts on the one purpose illuminated by my Soul's Vision.

Each moment is unique. The joy of seeking knowledge can be seen in the curiosity of a child. Each moment offers a fresh new adventure. Change is acknowledged as the Basis of Life. When engaged like a Lover, there is no beginning nor end. Just infinite potential.

In my first book "Timeless Love" I wrote about being adopted. There is an energy vibration with your name. By breaking down the limiting beliefs each aspect of my name holds, I can integrate both names for Soul Growth.

For example, The Energy of my name Jennifer M Maddy

Negative Beliefs v Positive Beliefs.

Denial of Spirituality. Highly critical of Self. Isolated. Insecure or choosing the opposite to be connected, intuitive, knowing, embody a high frequency. Be Balanced in male/female qualities.

The Energy of my Birth name. Maria Victoria O'Sullivan. (Birth name)

Negative Beliefs v Positive Beliefs.

Disempowered. Mistrusting. Disconnected from Spirit. Blocking of Power. Not Speaking Truth or choosing to embody being Strong, Stable, Peacemaker, Catalyst, Protected, Channel, Healer, Organised.

By integrating both names from my Soul Plan and choosing to learn and grow from my life experiences and SEEING my weaknesses as strengths, I AM more whole & complete.

Healing Affirmations.

I am fully supported and can only succeed, for my Soul knows only Freedom.

I build structure in my life to serve as a wise, emotionally resilient guide to others who seek truth and structure. I Love myself and my Soul shines through. I glow from Inside out. All of life comes to me with Ease, Joy and Glory. I am Victorious.

7. Moving into the 5th Dimension.

What is the 5th Dimension you ask? It's like shifting your car into 5th Gear. Inside each and every one of us, we hold a Spiritual GPS system, just like the GPS system in your car. Your spiritual GPS in your heart and soul. (Your Intuition) will guide you, as you journey through the Veils.

We are currently living in a third dimension reality. It is time now to move into a higher dimension and grow and evolve in consciousness. Bring the unconscious to consciousness, a shift in reality. Opening our eyes to a higher vision. An ability to see in the dark. These goals may seem way out of reach because of the world we live in presently, but maybe shifting into this reality will become possible hopefully over time. One step at a time. We have to walk before we run. Baby steps in spiritual awareness.

Glide with the Universe. Increased Awareness. Operate from your soul's essence. Your true self knows what it is you have come here to do in this lifetime. Fluid Movement. Effortless. Flow.

To embody the 5th Dimension, simply means to slow down, and act from authentic whisperings. Surrender to spiritual alchemy.

Believe and have experienced oneness and unity consciousness.

No Fear, You are safe. Lack of trust no longer exists.

You operate from Inner Guidance or your Intuition. You stop looking for answers from the outside world.

Trust the Universe.

Unity with everyone and everything.

A Higher Power, God/Goddess.

Connect to your own spirit team.

No need for physical pain which is a warning signal that you are still living in the 3rd Dimension.

Surrender ALL Control.

No Expectations.

All this is easy to say, hard to live.

Don't talk, if you can't walk the walk. Talking is easy.

Be Authentic.

Design Life Goals that are so perfect, they will take your Breath away.

Have an energy field that moves faster and is fluid.

Let's go into Oneness.

Navigate the Emotional Ups and Downs of the Journey.

Live in a state of Inner Soul Union.

Telepathically. Pick up on inner thoughts and feelings from others.

Re-Activation.

Ascension process. (Heaven is a place on Earth)

Interconnectedness

Unity Consciousness

Transformation. Self Cure (Feel Secure)

No Dis-Ease.

Magic Beyond Mindset.

Orchestrate a PLAN. (Goal Power by Matt Hunt) healthy food and games for children.

Goal Power by Matt Hunt. Goalpower.co.uk

"Jesus wishes for us, is always that we live life to the full. John 10:10.

Life in all its Beauty and Brokenness. It's never too late.

The number 10 is the number of completion in the Tarot Cards. Last year, I took time to study these cards with James Sweeney as my teacher. I highly recommend this Course. To be honest, I was afraid of Tarot Cards as you hear they tell you bad things. Truthfully, they really helped me open up more to energy and understanding myself. It changed my perspective. I still have so much to learn with these cards, but they are so interesting and I am in no rush. Everything in divine timing.

If you find yourself frequently seeing 1010 in your life, understand that this is not a coincidence and trust in your intuition that God is sending you a message. This is a sign of moving forward, and a reminder that you are on God's intended path. Because 10 holds such a strong vibration of new beginnings, creation and motivation. It is associated with the Divine. The perfection of Divine order. Knowing that God himself directs everything. Everything in your life is as it should be and is in perfect alignment and order.

Remember to honour God and yourself with your daily choices. See the bigger picture. In a world where you can be anything, be kind. Kindness is the best form of humanity. Humanity means caring for and helping others whenever and wherever possible. Humanity is helping others at times when they need the help the most, forgetting your selfish interest at times when others need your help and extending understanding and unconditional love to each and every living being on earth. To fulfil your responsibility and help someone else that needs your sympathy, your affection, your love during difficult times. Sometimes just being there, listening and holding someone's hand is enough for them to move through the pain. We can't take away their pain, and it's all part of life and life's lessons to go through the pain, but being sensitive and caring, full of compassion is key to helping them move through it.

Fill your own cup up first before you venture to help someone else. You can't help someone from a cup half full. Spiritual Selfishness is required. You are number 1. The most important person in your life. When you have strength to help someone else, do so from your heart. Be real and true to yourself first and then share your love. The 0 is a sign of eternity, evolution and infinity, since it looks like a circle. Everything comes full circle. The giving and receiving. All in perfect Balance. Give from a heart of gold, expecting nothing in return and the Universe will surprise you when you least expect it. Magic.

Mantra and words to use for Healing.

I step out of the way and surrender any need of control, in order to make room for God's healing love to flow through me and this situation.

Today, I count my blessings, small and large and I notice the new gifts that come to me from God. (make a list of all the things that you are grateful for. (the small and large things).

Faith. I have faith in God to heal this situation.

8. Connect to your Spirit Team

Over the past year, I have channelled messages from my own Spirit Team. Everyone has their own team in spirit who supports them on their journey. I believe my spirit animal for example is called Freddie the Fox. Freddie is an active listener. He loves to dance and enjoys new experiences. He helps me to remember my innocence and step back into my joy in life. During a meditation, or in a relaxed state of being, you can invite your spirit guides to step forward and meet them. At different times in our lives, we need different spirit guides to guide, direct, surround and protect us. Another one of my spirit team is Tony the Toad, he comes forward to help me with renewal and shedding the old skin to make way for the new. Mrs Kangaroo comes in with encouragement to look forward instead of dwelling on the past, to take big leaps forward and she shows me a clear picture. She teaches me to be determined and stay on the path I have designed for myself. She helps nurture my inner child and bring her out in my personality.

Would you like to connect to your Spirit Team?

Everytime I received a message from my spirit guides, I had to take TIME to integrate the energy. This has been challenging but very rewarding. Anyone who believes walking a spiritual path is easy, is wrong. We still get our triggers to work on but we see from a different perspective. Personally, this work brings me so much joy and ignites passion in my soul.

Healers are not perfect. They are actually far from it. Healers are people who have stared into the face of pain and suffering, and found themselves staring right back. They create themselves through all of the adversity and during the process, inspire others to do the same. Healers do not necessarily have to heal others. They heal themselves and inspire others to do the same.

Please enjoy the following messages which I received over the past year. I believe the following messages fit together like a jigsaw puzzle, joining together to inspire us. Please read and integrate aspects of the messages that trigger any emotions inside of you that come up to be released.

Messages from Higher Dimensions of Life!

Create movement in your life. E-Motion, Energy in motion.

Cancel clear & delete old outdated thought programmes & repeated behaviours in order to Reset your life and step into alignment with your own Source Light.

Angels are thoughts of God, who love for the sake of Loving. They bring Well-Being into our lives as they did in the time of Atlantis.

There is no such thing as Chance or Coincidence. Synchronicity is the Key. When situations or experiences come together to complete our lives.

Follow your own Intuition and inner Guidance.

Align your Chakras.

Climb out of the Rabbit Hole and live from a Higher state of Awareness.

Have Faith in Life. Take a Quantum Leap of Faith together as Light Workers and Live from our Hearts. Opening our Hearts to move into the 5th Dimension of Consciousness.

WAKE UP

The Kingdom of God is within.

Whatever you are thinking about, is in the process of BECOMING Choose to see Beauty in the World instead of Darkness.

Co Create with the Universe, it responds to your Intentions.

Friendship is so important. Be around Like minded people who raise your consciousness, earth angels and the higher beings of love & light and who live from truth.

Enlightenment

Lighting the way forward to develop Beautiful Souls Lead by example

Leave behind a Legacy you are proud of, for your children, grandchildren and all children whom you come into contact with. The young children are looking up to their elders for inspiration and guidance. They feel our energy. They know when we are sad and when we are happy. We cannot hide our feelings and emotions from them. All of our feelings and emotions blend into our Aura. Children see colour and energy.

Children are born with all these senses: It is us as adults that shut them down because of our misunderstanding. It's time now to allow the children to shine. Myself and Brenda also host children's workshops called 'Beams of Light, which are so gentle, and give children the basics for meditation, affirmations and connecting to their higher self.

Clairvoyant. Seeing Angels or Higher Beings of Light with your physical eyes or with your eyes closed.

Clairsentient. Feeling the presence of angels with sensations.

Clairaudient. Hearing the wisdom of angels through words or sounds in your inner voice.

Clairalience. A sense of smell.

Clairgustance. Clear tasting. Your intuitive sense of taste. Tastes from Spirit.

Claircognizant. A Knowing, A gut feeling. Psychic ability.

Wake up and smell the Roses and allow the children of our future to Blossom.

Coming out of the Darkness into the Light. Clear karmic ties. Set the stage for the actions of our life. Attract people, places and circumstances settings and situations to help you fulfil your Souls mission. Likened to Alice in Wonderland. Each opportunity gifts us a change to master situations and stop repeating patterns that do not serve your higher purpose.

In order for transformation to begin, I suggest you tap these mantas into your higher heart. Write a life of Manta's that fully serve you and your individual needs. Everyday add a new one.

Make this fun and colourful and open up your imagination and your creativity. Set yourself new life goals. Write them down and add pictures. Put a time frame on your vision board. This helps for your dreams to manifest and become a reality.

I put a time frame on writing this book. I had to send it to my publisher by 10/10 in order for it to be completed by 01/11, my mum Teresa Maddy's anniversary.

She will be 3 years gone this year. This is my 3rd book. The energy of 33 number sequences. This is a master number in Numerology. 33 is said to be one of the most spiritually inclined numbers, and that is why it is also known as the "Master Teacher". The Master vibrations of 33 are such that as the Kundalini force makes its way up the 33 segments of the spine, it opens all the Chakras that it encounters resulting in a tingling sensation in the body. Opening up the channel of communication.

We are the ones who are avid seekers and are naturally interested in gaining a lot of knowledge so that we can use it for the betterment of the whole of humanity and not just a personal agenda. We push our boundaries to explore the non-physical dimensions of life as well, which in turn helps us explore the Terra Incognita.

And all these number sequences have had a positive impact on my work. Just like our names hold an energy frequency, so do numbers. It's exciting noticing the signs from the universe.

We have been busy and recorded live videos for our websites over the past year and visited a lot of sacred sites in Ireland to feel the energy. All this work prompted the writing of this book to put all the messages together as an easy guide and reference. This work is part of our lineage. I am so grateful to be called forward to do this Soul Work.

Check out Author Eileen McCourt's book on Numerology. "You're just a number! And the Universe has it! Encoded within the Great Cosmic Code". Also check out our websites and our private Facebook pages, Declan Quigley, Brenda Coburn Murnaghan and myself.

Manta's

I release Resistance, I release heaviness, I am balanced. I choose instead to align myself with the word I speak and feel. It is safe for me to attract everything I need. I allow Abundance. I allow new opportunities. I am ready Now. I am Open. I am Crystal Clear. I am in Full Alignment. I am ready to receive it. I am feeling really good about myself and my Life. I Let go, I Let God. I trust every experience. I live my truth. I let go of Shame and Guilt. I forgive. I am confident. I am the Solution. I am Light. I am magnetic. I am irresistible. I am fully healed. I trust Spirit.

Connected & Balanced

Look at Life from a new Angle. Let Go, Let God.

You are the gatekeeper of your intuition.

 Put your Intuition Hat on.

Your prayers are manifesting. Remain positive and follow your inner guidance.

Hear the call to Spiritual rebirth. Ask to awaken to your Higher Self.

Be compassionate and humble to individuals less fortunate than you. Build a rainbow bridge to trust and understanding. Know that you are the bridge between heaven and earth.

Cut away negative attachments and address the need to be Right!!!

Transmute and Transform yourself.

Try to stop being rigid/chained by outdated belief systems.

Do not limit yourself. Be flexible. Be resolute in your convictions, faithful, loyal and constant.

There is no need for control or to be opinionated. Live life from your own awareness.

Have Courage during the hard time.

Be gentle to yourself always.

Set high standards for yourself and others that are within your reach.

Be Crystal Clear in your thoughts and actions.

Be able to say NO!!! If something does not feel right for you.

Go with the flow of life and be happy.

Live in the present moment awareness.

Have the ability to say YES!!!!! To Life.

Resolute leaders are highly determined and persistent. They embody inner strength and courage and they do not force their beliefs on anyone else. They are humble and not attached to others. They are happy in their own skin. They have a sense of self-worth. They know how to say NO and YES to life.

"I balance the masculine and feminine qualities that I embody" I am balanced in Mind, Body and Soul and so it is. Amen.

46

How does it feel to be enlightened? The best way to explain this word is to Surrender to Spiritual Alchemy. Surrender to the flow of life and life's experience. Some experiences feel like the carpet has been pulled from under your feet, and you are thrown up in the air and land upside down. Not all experiences are good but by integrating the good and the bad, allow for Soul Expansion. Whether your reality is heaven or hell on earth is down to your perspective, to what lens you're engaging your reality through. It's important to keep our eyes above the storm and focus on what is becoming and what we are creating rather than what is falling away.

"Everything we hear is an opinion, not a fact. Everything we see is a perspective, not a truth." Marcus Aurelius.

Breathwork is amazing

Lie down, make yourself comfortable and close your eyes. Relax your Body. Now breathe in for the count of 5, hold for 5 seconds and release to the count of 5. 555. This numerology sequence is also a message of Change/ Transformation. Be content to rest in stillness. When an emotion (energy in motion) comes up you don't run from this emotion but rather rest in the emotion. (Emotions come and go, just like an ocean wave ever evolving and dissolving). Let it go, and release. There is no place to go, no place to be, just give yourself time to be present to your own presence. This is the greatest present of all. A valuable priceless gift. Serenity. Own your own feelings and emotions. By embracing all of who you are, helps you to know who you truly are. An Enlightened Soul. A Being of Light. A Ray of Sunshine. Transmitting the 5th Dimension frequency as discussed in an earlier chapter.

INDEPENDENTLY TOGETHER (Our new Business) Brenda Coburn Murnaghan, Jennifer Maddy & David Connor.

Our new Enterprise is called. **Independently Together**. We collaborate together with other Holistic Practitioners and businesses to give you a broader scope of experience. The actual definition of Holistic means treating the whole person including mental and social factors rather than just the symptoms of a disease. With our Holistic Practice we envisage a new way of thinking, our aim is to educate people on modern day holistic approaches to wellbeing devoting time and resources to help you and the next generation to evolve, as Gandhi famously stated:" want to be the change in the world you want to see." I hope in the future you will visit us and let us help to enlighten and educate you. Remember you are the Healer of your life, and we are your teachers/mentors. We give you tools and coping mechanisms to help your Soul to grow and expand but we cannot do the inner work for you, that's your responsibility. We are not responsible, but we really do try our best to help support and encourage you.

The Swiss cheese analogy in relationships. Healing oneself takes multiple contributions, (the holes in cheese slices themselves) must be aligned for any adverse event to occur, as a sequence of events precedes it. This series of events can be changed. The barriers in our lives are likened to the slices of cheese and our weaknesses by the holes. Before any risk can manifest, multiple barriers must be breached for an impact in your life Multiple holistic treatments should be integrated to support you, which when mutually supported enables you to build on your personal relationships. Make a conscious choice to be the best version of yourself and think before you take action. Relationships come to trigger us to help our soul to expand. A relationship can go from ok to disaster in one step if we don't take responsibility for our own inner work and change our perspective if possible. The world will become a better place as a result if we choose.

A lesson truly learned is crystallised as earned wisdom. Wisdom helps you to recognise traps on the road and familiar patterns that you want to avoid. It also helps you to quickly gather information about where you are on your journey. It helps you to recognise your allies and know how to find the best route along the way. Sometimes, we have to cut people out of our lives who don't respect us. Would you keep drinking poison and allow people to treat you unfairly? You can block out pain from the past instead of dealing with the situations. This is likened to spiritual by-passing and in the long run, it catches up with you as you keep attracting the same experiences. Respect yourself. You are a unique child of God.

In our work as Holistic Practitioners, as we give, we receive also from every person we encounter and this also helps with our soul's growth and expansion. We look at alternative methods and solutions. Change is unstoppable. It's part of living. You get to choose if you live as a victim, rescuer, or abuser by looking at yourself and your behaviours and choosing to change to survive. It's your choice to acknowledge all parts of who you are. You do not have to self sabotage to be loved. Sometimes people don't change and it's not their fault either as they can only see out of the lenses they have in front of them, and they can't see that there is another way. I believe that once you recognise a learned behaviour, and why it keeps showing up in your life, then you have the ability to transmute it. (let it go) with compassion and integrity.

We surrender all control to a Higher Power and pray that you will see the Light.!!!!!!! Let's stand Individually Together and Breathe in The New Age and a new way of thinking. In God, we trust. We are mindful of the needs of people. We are here for you. Our aim is to educate you on modern day holistic approaches to well being, devoting time and resources to help you and the next generation evolve. Feel and breathe the love that you are.

The Truth has always been inside us. Encoded in our DNA. We have just forgotten our past lives. When we come into the world we come in as a crystal clear pure pristine clear diamond in our soul and over time your diamond (soul) becomes dulled and smudged by different experiences. By learning life skills and hearing other people's experiences as described in my second book, "We never say goodbye" you come to a realisation that everyone has lessons to learn and a story just dressed up as different experiences. This is Earth School. Our little souls incarnated here to learn.

Some Souls learn quickly and sadly for us depart to a New Dimension. And when they depart they leave a trail of fairy dust and love in our hearts that can never be forgotten. I believe that death brings liberation, as they are truly free of the constraints of the body. The soul becomes fully alive. There is nothing to fear as life is eternal. Be at peace. Time is a great healer and grief is one of our hardest lessons in life to understand.

Remember it's ok, to not be ok. It's ok to ask for help. You are not alone. Unless you ask you will never receive. Let go of struggle and limitations and review your life in order to transform it. Take inventory of your life and resolve to change, heal anything that's unbalanced. By connecting to your Higher Self, your Guardian Angel, Angels, Archangels, Spirit Guides, Lineage of Ancestors, past present and future, Human Angels and all Higher Beings of Light you begin to see things from a different perspective and angle. Be so close to God that you start to feel your Spirit come alive yet again. Not only do you start to live the next chapter of your life, but you discover what the next chapter is.

We clear your Aura, your energy body, chakra system, tap into your DNA with Sound Therapy and Vibrations, Tuning Forks, Gentle Touch, Meditation, Vision, Music, setting new goals, letting go and so much more to help you to come into remembrance of your true essence. LOVE. Coming into stillness. Stop doing and just be and feel the joy in your heart.

*Jennifer Maddy (right) & Brenda Coburn Murnaghan
with certificates for Archangel Reiki Master Teacher*

Messages from Archangel Chamuel!

The Archangel of Love
New Beginnings & a Fresh Start.

Believe in yourself by believing in God working through you.
Are you being truthful to yourself?
What are you attracted to?
Embody Unconditional Love.
Peace, Calm & Light.

Give yourself permission to bare your feelings and be vulnerable. Take down your barriers of protection from around your heart. Reveal to the world, who you truly are. Show your true Essence. Every single stage of development is perfectly likened to a beautiful rose. Just like a rose bud, plant the seeds, nurture them and watch them grow, break through the soil, and blossom all in divine time. Broken open. Expand and Grow. Radiate Beauty. Have self confidence through God's confidence.

The Rose is fathomless in its Beauty and in its meaning:
A Flower of great mesmerising beauty and intoxicating fragrance.

Let peace reign in your Heart. As it is already within your Soul which reflects Heaven. This is the turning of the tide, where healers are recognised at last.

Messages from Archangel Metatron!

Archangel Metatron offers you a second chance to live life from a higher perspective. Drop into your divine wisdom and higher intelligence. Please don't allow insecurities to hold you back. Be Crystal Clear and truthful to yourself, there is no room for lies or pretence as you are only lying to yourself. Try not to allow someone else to take over and rent a room in your head. Give yourself head space to think. Learn from life's experiences and step up into your power. Remember energy follows intention. Live from your own creative expression. Authentic and Real. Remember this is your life. You can't hit the replay button, so take back your power and choose wisely.

"Don't worry, be happy". Life will surprise you, prepare to be amazed. Live life in an all inclusive state of being. Put on your own crown.

Messenger of Emotions!

This is the beginning of a new emotional experience that could grow into something deeper. Envision amazing possibilities. See things from a different perspective. Embrace your uniqueness and allow it to serve you. Embrace Change. Choose which path to take. Get your bounce back in life. Embody a "Go with the flow attitude". Feel excited and full of energy.

Inner Child: Interconnectedness, effervescence and lightness, dreams the impossible, brings magic. The Inner

Child is an animating force through its full presence to the moment.

Inner Nurturer: Compassionate, soothing, peaceful, safe, mothering presence, able to behold their reality in appreciation which brings out the best in self and others.

Inner Sage: The inner sage perfects and refines life through its power of reflection and power to vision highest potentials. Inner sage perceives through eagle vision that can see the bigger picture around the details, and through eternal perspective that sees behind appearances. The inner sage brings depth and quality to life.

Inner Warrior: The inner warrior is our power to accomplish through action. It enables us to be self-determinative in life, knowing life to be our expression. Through cooperating with the moving forces of life in aware participation, yet as the appreciative observer, the inner warrior is our power to be fully in this world yet not trapped by it. It is the gateway of transcendence and our ability to live inner and outer realities as one.

Message from your Inner Child, by Sinead Rice, Family Constellations Facilitator.

You starved, but now you're full.

You bled, thought you were dying…..

You cried alone…. But I am here now, I see you.

You were suppressed… But now I hold you as you release.

You shut down… But now I open you up.

In the midst of the chaos, confusion, rage, sadness and despair. You didn't know but I do Breaking free to see what I see. You belong. It's Time. You are Safe.

Awareness

Discernment

Music

Embracing the elements.

To name just a few that make your light so bright.

You are not alone.

You've come so far.

I acknowledge you. I hear you. I see you.

We will unpack this slowly…

At our souls pace…

Together we are at peace.

Messages from Lord Melchizedek!

How can you make a Difference?

Declutter. Clean out the cupboards in your mind. Clean the windows of your soul, so that you see clearly the path that God has laid out in front of you. Invite the angels of declutter into your life. Renew your life to allow new thoughts, new ideas in your mind. Reset, rebirth, new growth. Flush out the toxins in your body, drink water, eat healthy and exercise. Trust that blessings are being bestowed upon you from God. Be gentle and kind to yourself. You are human, experiencing life in human form. Learn from your imperfections as they are part of who you are. Grow to Glow or Glow to Grow. Open new doorways and step through the doors. Embrace the future with an open heart. Have devotion to our Lady, and fully commit to your values, and relationships. Be clear about your next step.

Be your own lighthouse. I am the master of my fate, I am the captain of my soul.

Unfortunately, sometimes we lose our light warriors because they are switched off and suffer. Darkness can win the battle. We can lose battles, but we must not lose the war. Together we are strong. Be Brave. Allow the love of God to flow, waking us up as Human Angels.

Choose to be a Warrior of God's light. Carry the flame of hope and bring the light into all aspects of life integrating faith.

Messages from Our Ancestors!

Don't give up!!

Our souls are tired. Our ancestors who walk before us cheer us on from the sidelines. Thousands of lifetimes have passed before us ebbing back to the sea. Your presence creates a ripple effect in the ocean, the vastness of life. You are lifeforce energy, crystal sparkling radiant light vibrant and clear.

Realise you are Love, that which you have been seeking. Call off the search. Sometimes in the waves of change, we find our true direction, true north. You can make a difference, clearing, purification, vibrant life force energy. Be like a tiny Starfish creating a ripple effect in the ocean, the vastness of life.

Messages from the Archangels & Higher Beings of Light!

We are the lightbearers, the restorers, the guardians, protectors of the Holy Grail.

Together, let's plant new seeds of peace and love. Hope for our future as one great cosmic family. Let's flood the planet with light and release our shadows. Let's stand as a laser beam of healing light and claim our inheritance from our ancestors and release all traumas.

Before you start something new, you need to say goodbye to something that needs to be released. Let's tie up loose ends and complete this cycle together and strengthen our core values and beliefs. Set your intentions.

Allow a new pathway of healing and magic to unfold. Strengthen our immune systems.

Merge the meridians in your bodies and blend in synergy with Earth. Renewed, Vitality, Soul's purpose, Integration, Expansion, Branching out. Peace, Love, Hope & Blessings.

O' Great Spirit, Archangels & Higher Beings of light,
Raise Our Drums.
Mother Earth, Father God, All Directions.

Give us wisdom to encourage one another and lead by example, to teach our children, to forgive, to love, to respect one another. To be kind to themselves first and one another.
So that we may grow together in peace of mind, body, soul and spirit.
Merging as One.

Messages from Le Feile Bridgette!

Words of wisdom of St Brigid. She is the Celtic Goddess and Patron Saint of Ireland. We celebrate the festival of Imbolc, a festival of fertility and marks the beginning of Spring in Ireland. We have a holy well at St. Brigid's Shrine in Faughart just outside Dundalk and a sacred mural painted recently.

I live my true self in all its glory,
I release outdated story,
I step forward into my Joy,
Crystal Clear.
I am perpetual flame of honour,
I am the warm glow of Amber integrated with red jasper.

My heart is open, rejuvenated and bright.
Bathed in the Emerald Isle,
I am divine light,
I am inspired by equality, eternal patience, loyalty and alchemy.

I am balanced.
Exalted in Divine Love.
Connected universally with ONE BREATH
                          ONE PULSE
                          ONE HEARTBEAT

I embody the medicine within my Soul,
As I awaken to my True Life Story,
I live my true self in all its glory,
I release outdated story,
I let go of who I used to be,
I let go of my History.

Go raibh mile maith agat.

Your spiritual fire is growing within, It's an honour to celebrate our Celtic Goddess of Ireland. Call on Brigid to bring her sacred flames to clear stagnant energy and help us channel our energy into something that is important for our growth.

Message from the Elements!

Remember that you are Water,
Cry, cleanse, flow, let go.

Remember that you are Fire,
Burn, Tame, Adopt, Ignite

Remember that you are Air,
Observe, Breath Focus, Decide.

Remember that you are Earth,
Ground, Give, Build, Heal.

Remember that you are Spirit,
Connect, Listen, Know, Be Still

One cannot appreciate the majesty of Inner Peace without Deep soul healing. You are a gift. You have just been asleep. Open up to the Evolutionary changes happening on Earth. We are divine spiritual beings, multidimensional by nature. DNA activating.

Messages from Archangel Raphael!

The Archangel Raphael name means God has healed. He is one of the 7 Archangels who sit beside God.

He is the Archangel of rebirth, and the overseer of the Earth and magic of nature. He wishes for us to cleanse, and come into communion together and pray for our planet together in oneness. This is a time of great change and the turning of the tide. There is no room for separation. You are the healer of your life. You are in charge. You have the power inside you. It has always been there, like Doherty in the Wizard of Oz, all she had to do was click her shoes and she was home again. We keep searching for something on the outside to feel whole and complete and at home. How about, search inside. Easy does it. Gentle but so effective.

"I am helping you heal physical challenges in yourself and others, You are a healer, like me"

Prayer to Archangel Raphael.

Please help me to detach, retreat and let go so that healing can occur. Archangel Raphael enfolds us in his/her Emerald Wings of light so that we feel safe and supported as we follow our true path, so that true liberation can occur. This movement will usher in positive new energy and help us to go with the flow of life and reach our highest potential.

Dear God, and Archangel Raphael, thankyou for hearing and answering our prayers. Everyday we have an opportunity to pause, and consider where we are at this point in our life, and the direction in which we truly desire to go, and remain in the flow of the One Great Universal Energy we call God.

Messages from Quan Yin!

Quan Yin, our universal mother of all mums.

Our greatest strength lies within the gentleness and tenderness of our hearts.

This is an SOS to say sorry. I'm **SOS**orry.

Say sorry to yourself first, then each other and especially to mother earth, our planet. Quan Yin reminds us that we are held in the hands of unconditional love (love without conditions). Accept and embrace each other for the beautiful sparks of love, we truly are.

Quan Yin, the universal mother who never judges you, and continues to adore you.

Abundance is everyone's birthright.

Together let's hold the torch of light and lead by example, from our Hearts instead of our minds. Merging our mind, body and soul.

'You have to do what is right for you, no other person can fill your shoes, no matter what path you choose. Ignite the fire in your soul, transmute and clear

outdated thought patterns and become a positive source of energy. Hold the Light for others.
Let your Light Shine. Step into your True Self".

Message from Mother Earth!

How are we destroying ourselves and Mother Earth?

Know it's never too late to mend our relationship with Earth, with ourselves and others. It takes both compliments and criticism for us to grow, It takes both sun and rain for a flower or tree to grow. This is Duality.

Mother Earth, please help us to grow joyfully and be our authentic self in this world. Help us to be with you without pretence or hiding. We can sometimes fall into existing and doing rather than truly living. Mother Earth holds the ability to restore us. Please help us nourish and bring to life all parts of us that are deadened. Give us permission to grow, to enrich our lives, praying for freshness. Spring, Summer. Give us patience, in the same way that there are growth cycles required in nature, before we learn & grow. Allow Mother Earth to replenish your soul with her unconditional love freely. Take a great leap over & over again from existence to truly living.

Angels of the Violet Flame. (Transmutation)

As the seasons change, take Autumn for example. Watch the leaves on the trees turn to reds, yellow and orange and begin to wilt and die. Out with the old and in with the new. The new comes along and we must let go of the old, in order to make way for the new. Envision, the violet flame of transmutation clearing, clearing, clearing. Trust the process of life as like the leaves of a tree fall, we surrender and Let Go, and let God. To become vulnerable and naked and able to express ourselves like a tree in the winter. With an inner knowing that sometimes we need to shed our layers. (express our deepest emotions held buried deep inside.) Unroot, detangle and sprout new seeds of hope. New Life. New Ideas. New ways of living. Heal from inside out. Get the issues out of your tissues.

Open my eyes to see,
Open my ears to hear.
Open my heart to love.
Open my hands to touch.
Open my soul to expand

None of us know how much time we have left on this Earth. This is the circle of life. What is left in the end are our actions, the memories that you leave behind and how you made people feel. What you want people to remember you by is the Love you leave behind in their hearts. Love, Hope, Faith, Peace, Friendship, Courage, Memories, Eternal Life. If someone stops to hold your hand if possible as you take your final breath of life and they love you from the depths of their soul to your soul., isn't that an achievement.

Love, love, love. All we need is Love, no more pain or suffering, only peace and silence.

To Clear Stagnant Energy

Set the Intention for your highest good and highest healing for all concerned.

I hereby sever any vows of cutting the cords with my relationship with ………. That I made in this lifetime. I ask that all effects of these vows be lifted and undone in all directions of time.

And so it is, amen.

I invite Angels of the Violet Flame, Angels of the Violet Flame, Angels of the Violet Flame to cut and clear and transmute this outdated stagnant energy and allow it to dissolve into the Light.

Message from Dymphna Turley, Faith Angelz

"Let go and Let God,
Let go of your problems and let God handle them.
Let go of your hurt and let God heal you.
Let go of your fear and let God sustain you.
Let go of your worries and let God bless you.

Dymphna is a Faith Healer for Skin, Asthma and other conditions. Her devotion to God our father, Our Lady, All the Saints and Angels especially St Padre Pio, St Expedite, St Anthony is unwavering. So proud to call her my Soul Sister.

Prayer to Saint Pio, St Francis

Lord, make me an instrument of your peace,
 Where there is hatred, let me sow love,
Where there is injury, pardon.
Where there is doubt, faith.
Where there is despair, hope
There is darkness, light
And where there is sadness, joy.

Prayer to St. Expedite

Saint Expedite, now that I ask you, Saint Expedite now what I want of you, this very second. Don't waste another day. Grant me what I ask for. I know your power. I know you because of your work. I know you can help me. Do this for me and I will spread your name with love and honour so that it will be invoked again and again. Expedite this wish with speed, love, honour and goodness. Glory to you, St Expedite.

Godliness

This is a quality or practice conforming the laws and wishes of God. Devoutness and moral uprightness. To be wise is to live in godliness reflecting the nurture of the kingdom of God in the course of everyday life. Let go and let good, feel content which brings peace of mind and positivity that can facilitate growth and self improvement.

Message from Maura Baldwin. Dearest friend.

The Prayer.
I'll walk with God from this day on.
His helping hand I'll lean upon.
This is my prayer, my humble plea, May the Lord be ever with me….

The song is from "The Student Prince "operetta. Sung by Mario Lanza and made in 1954. Whenever times get hard, this is a beautiful prayer to hold in your heart. During times of change and transformation.

I welcome the High Priest into my life,
I welcome direction in my life,
I welcome guidance in my life. I hold the key in my heart.

Go out and have fun. Cut loose. Don't be afraid or hold back. Open your heart and celebrate. You are at the completion of a cycle. The Angels ask you to stop worrying and swim to clearer waters. You are held in the hands of grace. "Love Actually", movie. To me you are Perfect.

Message from Celine McGahon Byrne, Spiritual Medium

On the night of 2nd of September 2022, in Drogheda hospital, I stayed the night with my grandad who was very unwell. As I sat in the room, four beautiful Archangels appeared. The room lit up and shined so bright. Their names were Michael, Faith, Raphael and Azrael. The room was full of spirit, deceased family and friends of my granddad. I could feel the warmth and energy all around us. I knew when the time came, my granddad would be carried over to the other side. My grandad was never alone as he transitioned to spirit.

I was at home, when my grandad's spirit came to me to say goodbye. I knew he had passed before we got the phone call. My grandad passed away peacefully on the 5th of September. Song. (My heart will go on, by Celine Dion).

(Out of the Mind and into the Heart) by Eileen McCourt, Mary Magdalene Teaching.
Author, Teacher, Mentor, Guide and beloved friend.

Mary Magdalene urges us to come out of our heads and more into our hearts. To bring more compassion, more forgiveness, more caring, more gentleness, more harmony into our lives. And hence into our world!

To come back into your Body:

Mary Magdalene reminds us that our body is a beautiful temple for our Soul. A beautiful manifestation of the hand of God. A creator of life! Mary Magdalene urges us to get in touch with our own body, to embrace our own sexuality, to be happy in our own skin, no more guilt, no more criticism, no more judgement. Total acceptance of yourself exactly as you are now. Listen to your body's needs!

To come back into Oneness!

Mary Magdalene reminds us that there is no such thing as separation. All is One, One is All. And in the ONENESS, we have unlimited potential. It is only the ego that tells us we are separate and limited! Each one of us is in God and God is in each one of us! God is not any place outside of ourselves! Mary Magdalene urges us to accept our Divine Essence! Be still and know that you are part of God! You are carrying within yourself all the elements of the Godhead. Be still & know that I am God.

To come back into the Here & Now!

Mary Magdalene urges us to accept that the present, the here and now, is the only place we can ever be! Living in the present means being fully aware of everything around you at this moment in time, and that is what being alive really means. This is living your life! Experiencing the here and now with all your physical senses.

To come back into Trust!

We have placed our trust in all the wrong places. Mary Magdalene now urges us to come back into trusting in the Universe, in the Great Divine Plan for humanity, trusting the Universe to deliver what is for the highest good of all, to not worry or fear, to connect with Source, to live in Trust that all is being taken care of by a Greater Intelligence.

To come back into Truth!

Mary Magdalene urges us to come back into the truth of who and what we truly are! To accept our own God Essence, to live our lives honestly as each and every one of us wants to, and has the right to live our own life, and not restricted or suffocated by the dictates of society or any controlling creeds or beliefs. To allow our soul to fly freely and to sing its own song, and to allow others to do the same.

To come back into Nature!

We are surrounded by so much beauty and magic in our world! Beauty is everywhere. Magic is everywhere. Mary Magdalene urges us to come back into Nature, to spiritually indulge ourselves in the great healing power of Mother Nature. To escape from the fragmented living in which so many are now finding themselves. The spirits of Nature, the spirits of the land all around us, waiting for us to connect.

To come back into your Inner Goddess!

There is an inner Goddess, the feminine, within each and every one of us. Mary Magdalene now urges us to release that inner Goddess, to awaken our spirit, to remember the unlimited potential each and every one of us has to transform our suffering world for the better. It is time to release our inner Goddess in the form of caring, kindness, compassion, nurturing, nourishing, gentleness, tolerance. It is time to radiate our inner Goddess out all around us!

To come back into your own Spiritual Light!

Mary Magdalene reminds us that if only we could see ourselves as the Higher Beings of Light see us, each of us a bright shining light, then we would not hesitate to shine our Light out to all humanity. Each of us is unique, Each of us is an individual expression of our creativity of the one great universal energy we call God. God in physical manifestation!

Awesome in our greatness, Unlimited in our potential.

To come back to Love!

Mary Magdalene reminds us that God is Love. God is everything and everywhere and so love is everything and everywhere.

Love simply means seeing yourself and everyone else as the pure bright spiritual beings we all are, and so therefore, we do not judge, we do not criticise, we do not condemn. We accept all differences and diversities as part of the great creation.

To come back into your heart!

Mary Magdalene reminds us that your head is controlled, manipulated in so many ways. But your heart is free! Listen to your heart!

This is the time for the merging, the marriage of the sacred masculine mind, the sacred feminine heart, your divine masculine and your divine feminine, in order to bring about the new age for which humanity has been waiting for so long.

Cleansing of stagnant energy on The Hill of Tara with Jennifer Maddy, Eileen McCourt and Brenda Coburn Murnaghan to create Clearer New Energy for future generations.

We recorded this meditation under my Sacred Pyramid (A Soul Temple) in Dundalk to enhance the healing to a higher vibration. The pyramid is magnetic and magnifies the energy. I am so grateful to be called to do this Soul work as part of a collective consciousness. Together we are strong, and can make a difference. Each one of us is dedicated to bringing change to society and we all have our unique qualities combined.

Our Sacred Pyramid in Dundalk, Co Louth. Private one to one treatments available by appointment

My Own Messages from Mary Magdalene! Teacher Awakens

As we unite together under our sacred pyramid, in Dundalk, we are reminded of our divine spark of energy. The Buddha Maitreya, Christ's meditation pyramid, helps align the awakening of the Soul and brings an integration of your body, mind and spirit through personal and planetary healing and soul therapy.

Geometrically designed in order to bring about an alignment of the planet and our spiritual abilities. This pyramid is a very divine sacred geometric design. As a human being, even a tree or flower has this design. It can awaken inside of you. You will have God's mind. God's emotions and you will see God in the World.

To become conscious is so much different than to become positive. To become conscious and aware, we must become authentic, authenticity includes positive and negative. (Teal Swan). To heal is to experience the opposite. You decide your 'habits' and your habits decide your future. You get to choose. Come visit our pyramid and decide yourself. Take that leap of faith and experience yourself……..

May all the beauty that has died in you come back to Life, as you take back your Power.

A shift from the mundane to the sacredness of all life by gaining a new perspective.

We value your feedback after experiencing a Soul transformation.

Crystal Clear pure energy resides within each of us, it's simply the time now to remember our true essence. You have something important to share. Follow your inner call. Don't let anything stop you. Step into your rebel heart.

Above, below, we ignite the Fire within our Soul,
We place Light Crystals in a Grid around our Aura and draw
All of our Divine Energy back within.
DIVINE INTEGRATION

Align me now with my inner divinity.
Through my own free will as a being of light.
I allow my merkaba to alight.
Arising from below and descending from above,
I surrender!

Step Up!
Ignite your flame.
Awaken & Arise
Awaken in Spirit.
Welcome your Twin Flame.

Divine Woman
The Womb of a woman.
The seed of a man.
Birthing the 5th Dimension.
The Golden Age.

Message from Angels & Heart of God.

We create a stargate for the healing and release of the Souls and negative energy caught between the dimensions of heaven and earth. May the gate we create with our combined love be a shining star to guide lost souls home. Merge into union the energies of heaven and earth. May the Stargate be used as a pathway for the healing and union of heaven and earth within our hearts.

The Star Gate Technique uses the energy of angelic and human hearts, connected to the heart of God and the heart of the Earth to create a bridge. Within our hearts exists a sphere of energy that vibrates with the energy alignment of unity. The Star Gate Technique creates a permanent sphere of energy identical to our unified heart sphere as a gateway. This technique can be performed by highly evolved Souls (Master Instructors) like ourselves, who understand spiritual work to a high degree and have mastered our own spiritual evolution and are experienced in this line of work. There is a protocol that needs to be followed. You must state your intention clearly and give specific details. For example, Star gates are perfect for hospitals, churches, and the room of a dying person. They can also be used to heal past events such as war situations and catastrophic world events. Energy follows intention. Just like our prayers.

This work is heart based and full of love. We are honoured to be called. We are surrounded in a bubble of protection and love. A stargate is a shining star lighting the way home and a return to love. In the future, we hope to create this Sphere of Love for humanity to merge together as One. No more war, hatred or fighting. Let Heaven be a place on Earth. And so it is. Amen.

Ascension Process! **New Beginnings, New Age. Circle of Light. Embrace the Adventure of Life!**

I chose the cover of this book "Let go, let god" as a Mirror reflection of life. The swans are a symbol of two becoming one surrounded by so much sparkle and light. The reflection is similar to the number 8. 8 is the number of infinity and beyond. The lotus flower is a symbol of resurrection. The lotus flowers open their petals with the rays of the sunlight and again close their petals at sunset. The spiritual meaning of the flower is rebirth and resurrection. The three meanings of the lotus generally represent spiritual awakening, purity and faithfulness. Light & Darkness. Even in darkness, focus on the light above, below and within. The purple represents wisdom, dignity, devotion, peace, pride, mystery, independence, ambition, creativity and magic. The words let go, let God represent Goodness.

Life is Wonderful

I shine my Light

I am In LOVE

I Reclaim my Power.

I am the master of my Life.

I am a magnificent BEING of Light.

I love and respect myself

I am worthy I am Beautiful I am adaptable.

I am compatible.

Expansion of Happiness is the purpose of Creation and we are here to enjoy and radiate happiness Everywhere.

Trust you live in a world of abundance and all is well, perfect whole and complete.

Trust yourself: The past is written. The future is yet to come and all you have is the present.

"Our lives are all different but yet the same" by Ann Frank is still relevant today.

It is important for us to value inclusion and adversity and accept those who are different to us. We wish to live in a world where we are safe and free regardless of race or religion.

I love having my relationship with the spirit world and higher beings of light. It brings so much peace and new adventures. You never know where you will be asked to go. I try to live in the present moment, and value everyone whom I come in contact with. I give them my attention and love during these interactions.

Life is Wonderful. "It's a wonderful life." film by Frank Capra's. Highly recommend it. Value how your life affects other people. Sometimes we just do not realise how important of a role that we play.

I personally try to balance my work, time, energy, diet, exercise, play etc and have intimate relationships and have fun along the way. I am certainly not perfect by any means, and I know I still have a lot to learn.

I am a Leo (Lion). Ask my good friend Karen Binks what my traits are. Karen's website is Seeker of Truth. Karen is an inspirational guide, friend and teacher in my life and also a Leo. She is 3 days older than me and jokes that I pushed her off the cloud before me. The relationship that myself and Karen have is powerful. Opposites attract. We work from a different point of view. Karen works with the Shadow self (which is integrated emotions and feelings from the past that bring you into the present), and I work with the Light and the Angels and the higher beings of Light which is similar, but we use different methods to become a better person.

Karen and I complement each other and balance our work with long discussions, not always agreeing but respecting the values of our work. We both have the same core beliefs to align ourselves and others to be connected, grounded, resilient and aware of their highest potential.

We believe in ourselves and our Gifts and encourage each other to soar.

Sometimes, I say things that hurt other people unintentionally and unknowingly to myself as we all do, as the words come out of my mouth before I think. They say, think before you speak. And sometimes, people hurt me with their words and actions too. I have to remember that the ball is in my court and I have a choice to dwell on this energy or experience or be the bigger person and move on and let it go. To be honest, I find animals easier to understand than humans. Lol. A great way to clear negative people (energy) from your life, is to imagine them floating away on a cloud and dissolving into the distance. Not everyone is here to stay in your life, some come for a day, a month a year or a lifetime. And that's ok. If you have one true friend in life, you are blessed. Treasure them. Forgive easily.

To Become Versatile. Continue to seek, until you find. The kingdom of God is inside of you and outside of you. Recognise what is in your sight and that which is hidden from you, will become plain to you. For there is nothing hidden which will not become manifest and nothing covered will remain, without being uncovered. Ask yourself, what is my purpose? How do I overcome my challenges? Do not do what you hate to do. (relationships, job, home etc). Stop resisting change. Speak as though you have something already. Feel the energy and vitality. Advance and take control.

Dreams do come through, when you believe. Aim higher. Let go of self doubt and reach to the Stars with your dreams and desires. Live in a spirit full of inspiration. Reclaim your power, if you have lost it or given it away especially to addiction, or loss of identity in whatever manner. Become your own master. Do the inner work. Feel whole and complete again. Reunite your head, heart & spirit with a golden thread of light. Know that you are in the process of becoming and have the power to hold the whole world in your hands. These are golden nuggets to freedom.

Say & feel these words & integrate them daily into your belief system.

Look in the mirror and repeat them to yourself and reflect them back to you.

I am healed.

I am in full alignment with my source of light energy.

My life has meaning and purpose and I know which direction to go forward.

I am willing to be in my Contract now for my highest good and highest healing. I open the door to infinite potential.

I am a VIP (very important person)

My inner light is my greatest strength and wealth.

I am a magnificent being of Love and Light.

I am in charge of what happens in my life.

I am in control.

I am supported.

I am organised.

I love & respect myself.

I am worthy.

I am beautiful.

I glow from Inside out.

I know that I am pure spirit.

I am universal

I trust Inspired Action.

I attract situations and experiences that honour my Soul.

I expand my Love & Joy.

The only way is forward.

A new chapter of my life begins, I let go of fear and embrace the unknown.

I am resilient and my spirit is powerful.

Some Power Crystals for Chakra Clearing and strengthening Spiritual Connections.

Amber

One of my favourite crystals is Amber. Amber is a powerful healer and cleanser of the body, mind and spirit. It clears depression, stimulates the intellect and promotes self confidence and creative expression. It encourages decision making, spontaneity and brings Wisdom, balance and Patience. Brings so much joy and warmth. Likened to the Sun. Pure in Undiluted form as it is a fossilised resin

from evergreen trees. Cleansing and renewing. Carries knowledge of millions of years.
Calming

Turquoise Crystal
This powerful Crystal strengthens the connection to Mother Earth and helps carry your prayers to God.

Empowerment, Understanding. Best for leadership qualities, clear communication. Prosperity and success.

Selenite Wand. Higher Realms
Reflects light fallen directly from the moon.

Spiritual Growth. Personal transformation, Peace. Aligns the Aura and Energy Field.

Crown: Clear Quartz
Works on any conditions. Stone of Power. Protects against negativity. Connect to your higher self. Align and clear your body, mind and spirit.

Third Eye: Amethyst/ Fluorite
Stone of concentration. Absorbs neutralises negativity. Balances our energies. Promotes Psychic Development.

Throat Blue Kyanite / Light blue Angelite
Helps stimulate the birth of psychic gifts & connection with Spirit Guides.

Heart: Atlantisite//Rose Quartz
Self-discovery. Encourages feelings of love and compassion. Wonderful meditation stone. Enhance a sense of security and establish personal relationships and boundaries.

Solar Plexus Yellow Citrine/Orange Calcite
Enlightenment, Optimism, Success, Enthusiasm, Happiness, Clarity.

Sacral: Red Jasper
Supreme nurturer. It sustains and supports times of stress and brings tranquillity and wholeness. It provides protection and absorbs negative energy. It balances yin and yang.

Grounding: Black Kyanite
Favourite among energy healers. Can be placed on any chakra to send healing energy to any tears or holes in the chakras or aura. Its fan shape can help to sweep away any unwanted energies. Great stone for attunements and meditation. Brings vision & clairvoyance.

Himalayan salt lamp
Every home should invest in one of these. Clears negativity. Calming.

Mystic Merlinite
This Crystal will directly resonate with your Soul's Blueprint, awakening Ancient Light codes for your whole being. Divine Composure. A new pathway to be a human angel.

Some of my Favourite Angels/ Archangels.

Song, 100 thousand angels at my side, song by bliss.

Michael, Strength/Protection/ Release Negativity/ Confidence/ Clarity.

Raphael, God Heals/ Healing/ Wellbeing/Forgiveness/ Protection/ Emotions/Miracles

Gabriel, Communication/New opportunities/Skills/Inner Child Healing/Faeries/Creativity

Uriel, Joy/Understanding your Dreams/ increased intuition/

Jophiel, God's Beauty/Creativity/Beauty/Art/Hope/Joy

Ariel, Light of God/Earth Warrior/Heal the Earth/Serve the planet/Animals/Contribute to making this world a better place to live in.

Haniel, Joy of God/Warrior/Courage/Healthy Boundaries.

Chamuel, Love, creating and manifesting your big vision, movie of your life/serenity

Metatron, Divine Intelligence/Teacher/Leadership/Effortless/Magnetic Energy Great with children.

Sandalphone, Angel of Music/Presents people's prayers to God/Inspires you to use your talents that God has given you.

Azrael, Gatekeeper. Guide over the Rainbow Bridge/Souls arriving and leaving this planet.

Zaphkiel, Knowledge of God/Sacred key to abundance/symbol chalice/Holy Grail/great for exams and study.

Zadkiel, /Success/Gratitude/Breakthrough Abundance Blocks/Create Wealth to be able to give from the Heart/Recycle/Transform/Reuse.

Raziel, Mystery Bucket. Give up the need to know. /hidden gifts/past lives/ Dissolve what no longer serves you.

Sarah, Empowerment/attract new opportunities people places settings and situations that I need to shine in my life.

Faith. Fate/Freedom of Choice.

Jeremiel, Life Review/Akashic Records/Library of your Soul/Branch out to new possibilities. Motivational speaker, teacher, leader.

Nathaniel, Pure Soul/Gift of God/Restorer of Faith in God/ Inner Kindness.

Let Go, Let God

This is the movie of my life. I am the Lead Actress. (Star). Every person I met in life are the main characters. There is no repeat. You have only today, yesterday is gone, and tomorrow is yet to happen.

I can replay memories in my mind, but over time, I forget the important details, so by writing this book (my story) trilogy, not only helps me remember, but leaves a "handprint" to be remembered along my path.

Everything I want is already here. I am a communicator. I am highly intuitive and sensitive. I speak my truth and use my voice and write from my heart. I am a leader in my own right. I boost morale and build team spirit. I am a vast ocean of energy. I glow my true colours. Hope transforms into a faith that God has a beautiful plan.

I am charismatic. Archangel Michael and Gabriel work with me. Together with Angel Uriel, the yellow joy and ray of sunshine, bright light and full of happiness. I ask the Angels to vacuum all negative energy from my being. I complete a 360 degree angle to come home to feeling loved, accepted, for "Who I am". My energy field is magnetic, full of light.

Who are you?

Our Soul Work together as part of a Team over the past years has been cleansing out the old energy into new light energy. Each time we recorded a live video for Facebook, we personally integrated the energy into our lives. This has been an amazing year of change, and we are only truly beginning to understand how valuable our soul work is. We as lightworkers embrace these changes. We must ground our Divine sparks of divinity in order to manifest our vision and bring our souls mission to life.

Hopefully, I will write many more inspirational books in the future from amazing life experiences that are yet to come. But for now, I thank all the characters for showing up on my path to Enlightenment. Remember you don't need good luck when something's written in the Stars. We are destined for greatness.

To Cross Over. Trust your own opinion.

Let Go, Let God

Namaste. (The light in me honours the Light in you)

And many Angel Blessings from our Hearts to yours.

Dove of the Holy Spirit

Necati Sahin
+90 0530 9470567

Printed in Great Britain
by Amazon

11392168R00061